THE SINGER OF ALLEPPEY

THE SINGER OF ALLEPPEY

poems by

Pramila Venkateswaran

Shanti Arts Publishing
Brunswick, Maine

THE SINGER OF ALLEPPEY

Published by Shanti Arts Publishing
Interior and cover design by Shanti Arts Designs

Shanti Arts LLC
193 Hillside Road
Brunswick, Maine 04011

shantiarts.com

Image on cover and in interior is of the author's paternal
grandmother; artist is the author's sister, Jayashree George.

Printed in the United States of America

ISBN: 978-1-947067-39-4 (softcover)
ISBN: 978-1-947067-40-0(digital)

Library of Congress Control Number: 2018940223

For Sitala (1895-1969), my paternal grandmother, singer and composer, whose compositions were not preserved, and about whom I know very little.

ACKNOWLEDGMENTS

Some of the poems in this volume, with slightly modified titles, have appeared in the following journals and anthologies:

A Taste of Poetry: "Yogurt"; **Adanna**: "Kitchen Years" and "Autumn"; **Bards Annual, 2015**: "Karma Blues"; **Block Island Poetry Project Anthology**: "Boy-Man" and "Margaret Sanger"; **Confluencia In the Valley**: "Letter to Sarojini"; **Contemporary Poetry—An Anthology of Present Day Best Poems**: "Ode to the December Flower"; **The Dance of the Peacock**: "Ruled by Proverbs" and "The Chatterbox"; **Draw Me Inmost** (Stockport Flats, 2009): "Single, 1947"; **Glint Literary Journal**: "Paean to Saraswati"; **Grabbing the Apple**: "The Long Shadow of Evil." **Kalyani Magazine**: "Meditation on Rain in Ragam Mohanam" and "Boat Song"; **Long Island Quarterly**: "Alleppey Mornings," "Crayons," and "A Wife Responds to the Photographer"; **Long Island Sounds Anthology**: "Youthful Evening"; **Muse India**: "Ambi Practices Tamil Vowels on his Slate," "Tryst with Death," "After the Funeral," and "Indigo"; **Obsession: Sestinas in the Twenty-first Century**: "The Art of the Invisible"; **Two Review**: "Art by the Way"; **String Poet**: "Kummi Dance"; **The Writing Disorder**: "Sex," "Oiled Hinges," and "Ancestral House, Alleppey."

I would like to thank Pat Falk, Kathrine Jason, Sally Drucker, Richard Newman, Carmen Bugan, Patti Tana, Rosie Wiesner, and Gladys Henderson for reading and commenting on some of the poems in this volume.

I am grateful to Nassau Community College for granting me a sabbatical to work on this book. My immense gratitude to my sister Jayashree George for contributing her art work for the cover.

To my relatives who shared their stories of my paternal grandmother, Sitala, which helped me recreate her life in poetry, many thanks.

Also, thanks to my husband Ramu and my daughters, Aditi and Amrita, for supporting my writing life.

Pramila Venkateswaran

CONTENTS

NOON

EVENING

Midnight

Dawn

The Long Shadow of Evil

The hall spins, bride, groom, flowers,
guests, husband. Then routine happens.

Do I have all the ingredients
for the feast?

A bird bangs itself against glass and falls.
That's how I feel when he slaps my face.

Spirit, better not stand me up, I yell
silently. This is how surprise springs and settles,

wordless bitterness in my throat,
his causeless rage twisting him ugly.

I know the difference between sinking dark
and womb dark: My marriage is dung,

I choke, marriage is dung dung dung.
Singers croon *sita kalyanam vaibogame*

Rama kalyanam vaibogame
as bride and groom walk around the fire.

Roses on the nuptial bed, stitched into garlands,
roses perfuming waters anointing the wedded pair.

I place my hands on my truth-telling heart
thud-thud thud-thud, I close my eyes, the hall spins.

His rage, my humiliation, then the pretense,
laughter and gossip, the rippling of everafter,

symbols of fertility mocking me: twin hills of lentils,
clay pots filled with new sprouts, babies

placed on the bride's silken lap, the circle
of fire redrawing her womb.

My husband's father and his father's father,
their anger, a fiery chain, will dog my sons.

How will they pick their paths
through evil sown by ghosts?

My dead mother calls, *Sitala, tune up the strings,*
before your mind dulls and bells drag you to duties.

His words, I'll-die-and-only-then-
you-will-regret, I tune out.

Mother visits in dreams, *Sing your heart out,*
you're wedded to words till your tongue is ash.

Night

Ancestral House, Alleppey

That which you want to stay hidden,
the house shakes awake: commands,
suddenly silenced singing, men's
stomps, muffled cries, quiet after rain.

Shadows of its many doors darken
my mind, reflect roadside lanterns
swinging to the pulse of shadows
flitting across the walls

awakening ghosts of cooks, gardeners,
kids playing catch, women drying
their hair,

he who wrung his wife's eyes dry.

Hear him walk through the arched
entrances hollering to figures behind
pepper vines, spreading his legacy.

WAITING FOR THE PHOTOGRAPH

I await her, as I gaze at seagulls chasing the wake stirred
by goslings following their elders toward water;

how will she look, this woman who barely
grazes my memory? Will she be earth-colored,

with dangling breasts, mussed brown sari,
ornament-bare, *mooli*,

as mother would say about me
when I refused to wear jewelry? Or will she be

a young woman gazing into the light,
as if sitting for an exam, jet eyes, hair pulled into a plait,

dark face, sweat beads above the upper lip, a diamond snug
on the right side of her nose, ear studs, gold chains,

a red dot on the forehead, silk blouse, purple sari gathered
over left shoulder? I kick at seaweed snaking the shore line,

so stark the contrast of memory and imagination.

COME, DANCE WITH ME IN THE RAIN

I want to twirl around
in the rain that's pouring perfume,

twirl and sing
like the champak and hibiscus dripping their
dye.

I want to rub this song into the earth,
cup handfuls of wet mud and drink its smell
till my mind explodes like an alcoholic's.

Look at me dance,
my pirouettes have peeled the skin from my soles.

I do not want to hear commands of
don't get wet, you'll catch a cold, carry an umbrella.
O, send the servant to buy the fruit.

I *will* get wet and catch a fever
and be happy I danced in the rain pouring,
pouring like an insane waterfall.

ELECTRICITY COMES TO ALLEPPEY

No more do I see
hurricane lamps flickering
in and out of trees

or follow the mystery
swaying up the road
into darkness

or watch others reappear
milling about like fireflies

or hear the creak of one
swinging on its hook

smell the burnt wick
swell with oil and burst
into a tall petal of flame.

Kummi Dance[1]

It's evening. Lamps are alive. Temple bells ring.
I sashay out in a bright red skirt and a zari top.
Sukanya, Radha, and Paddu run to meet me in their finery:

Skirts flying, we dance in a circle, clapping
as we move our hips, and twirl — plaits flying,
steps beating the earth awake to bells and song.

Clap, clap, clap, we dance the kummi,
the whole land claps the kummi round and round.

We call our sweethearts, the ones promised to us,
to fill us with joy, more passion than we know;
soon it will be time to wear our mothers' wisdom.

Clap, clap, clap, we dance the kummi,
the whole land claps the kummi round and round.

We are birds widening the sky of earth, feet flying,
skirts skimming the ground, anklets ringing,
faces bathed in jasmine and sweat,
breath in our bodies bursting the hooks
holding our blouses in place.

Clap, clap, clap, we dance the kummi,
the whole land claps the kummi round and round.

---

1. popular folk melody of South India sung and danced to during
festival seasons

HUSBAND

Everyone calls him handsome
women on the street stare
they say he is an angel who lost his way
they memorize him

I see what they don't
the invisible thing   like the heart's shadow
anger that coats
his words that emerge from their mine

If I looked through a telescope   like the photo I saw
in a recent newspaper on his desk
of a European model of a lens
it will enlarge   evil gathering in him like a cloud of vermin

I would pick apart

antennae
filament
wings
snout

Autumn

I'm pregnant
again   this is my eighth
but this time it's different

This morning the river the mango and jackfruit
branches heavy with shadow last night's rain
fresh on the path   this baby makes the world new

Behind me the cashew groves stand taut
I venture into them   receive
a handful of roasted cashews
in their pink-and-brown lined skins
from a woman's smooth dark hands

She in blue top and white mundu melts
into the deep cool where winds whistle
as I lift my hands to my face to smell
his fair baby skin

His coal black eyes and his smile
don't ask me how I know
will charm   make me want to live

Boat Race

The boats are launched, the fishermen's bodies are alert,
oars poised. Whistle. A flock of crows shoots up, air unlocks,

the fleet torpedoes into the swimming light.
The air is thick with song, feet tap to the swish of oars

and voices. I open my wet palms and wipe them on my sari.
Sweat beads decorate my forehead, race down my face.

My heart quickens as bodies crane to glimpse the winning boat.
The song of the rowers coils around my brain,

my blood a crazy drum, faster than the rhythmic beat
of percussion on the shore cheering the rapid oarsmen,

thom-thom thom-thom thom-thom thom-thom.

I am hanging on to the ledge of explosive clapping
as men spill out of catamarans, merge into a crowd

that knows how spirit wrests itself from the body.
Relatives scatter, the women are gathering their kids

and heading home, turning their backs to water
transforming into fish or fowl in the gloaming.

DIDN'T I TELL YOU IT WILL BE A BOY?

1

As the midwife slides him out
easy—five births later—
I see his buttery skin
between her dark fingers.

Cord cut. I receive him
count one two three four five
six seven eight nine ten toes,
fingers, is he breathing?
She slaps his side and he
wails *I am your son.*

His father stands at the door
happy his line's secure:
an offering from the blue god himself
his very name, also his playthings,
rubber ring, shell, pet snake.

I offer my son a pet name, Ambi,
to yell a chore, call down a prank.

2

Ambi is a plant I pour
sunlight on. Shadows still
in the distance

later loom in his father's mind
clouding the secret mantra he whispers
into his son's ear,
may divine illumination
awaken our wisdom,

wraps the sacred thread
across the young body perspiring
from smoke swirling from the flames
carrying the father's wish to the gods
make my son in my image.

Ways to Relieve Routine

A roomful of men in pure white veshti,
sacred threads across their smooth brown chests

chant the Vedas — a whisper in their ears
now an ocean heaving above the town's watermark.

Astrological charts, auspicious times,
stars, cosmic designs fill their fists.

They drink up holy water spooned
into their palms, sprinkle their heads with it,

go out into the night to their mistresses
before heading home to their wives.

BIRTHING

My scream is a knife stabbing the midwife's hands
        wild buffaloes on a rampage

yelling *fuck you* to the power of infinity
        a banshee calling her tribe

My scream is swifter than light
        a swirling tide rising in seconds

breaks up lightning
        crumbles meteors to dust

It is the stench of blood
        bursts like angry rash on baby skin

My scream wrenches neutral light, bends it like metal
        pushes walls, bleeds a river

bleaches the dark
        rousts the dead
tosses boulders down a ravine
        twists benedictions into curses

        My scream grieves and grieves

LULLABY TO WARD OFF DEATH

All my babies are born beautiful.
I can't tell how long they'll live.
I can only pray they outlive me,
not die when they are nursing,

or when I'm shaking the rattle
and tickling their soles to hear them
giggle like tiny brooks, or kissing
their pudgy cheeks when they find me
hiding behind a chair or a door.

I sing *kaiveesu amma kaiveesu,*
kadaiku polam kaiveesu, picking up
their little arms and swinging them
back and forth, imitating the stylish young.

When my fingers shape stars falling from the sky
or fruit from the trees, their eyes are unswerving
from the descending stars, falling fruit,
familiar hands that rock them to tranquility.

I believe I can keep death away when they breathe
mother scent, taste my sour skin and snuggle
into the folds my body makes to shelter them,
helping them grow muscle by muscle
listening to me sing them to dream.

Morning

Art by the Way

Imagine if the dye had to be made,
leaves and flowers plucked, mixed
with water and stirred over a hot stove

cooled under the moon, the right branch
found and sharpened to dip into the potion,
a piece of parchment, dry enough

but not too dry, has to be smoothed
before the pen can be lifted
from the decoction, wet enough

but not drippy, so the words form in neat,
thick chunks as the hours pass slowly,
so at day's end if four lines are written

it's a feat, especially if dishes have to be washed,
laundry hung out to dry, kids fed, and
a hundred pieces of family life picked up:

it must have been the woman with magic
who put a god on watch to brush a few strokes
on leaves, the pen's spout, her life, so imagine

the women who couldn't manage it all,
let the dye coagulate, the pen stick to the bowl,
the parchment vanish into yellow dust.

Ambi Practices Tamil Vowels on His Slate

Umbrella, quick, get me one, Ambi yells,
Awkwardly running back from the gate,
Its rusty hinges screeching as it swings open.
Eating hurriedly as usual, I say, handing him his umbrella,
Uttarkhand isn't where you are headed, nor
Ooty, just school around the corner.
Anyone seen my slate? he asks, dripping, ready to dash.
Ay, wait, here it is, hurry, you'll get sick,
I say, loving his jet black hair, his quick jump
Over a puddle, his lithe form, his fair skin.
Oh, and don't get your homework wet, I yell.
Out of pain joy, say the great ones who delineated
Akshara, u, aa, i, ee, from rain beat, my son's heartbeat.

Alleppey Mornings

I walk sweat beginning on my brow

my feet steadily moving down the high sidewalk
tracing the footsteps of my grandmother
toward the boats behind a scrim of wild plants

It's early   the sky already blue
reaching for white

the road leading to Mullakal temple
absorbs a few men and women
a couple of school girls in uniforms

a cart two autorickshaws
speeding down

a bus stopping comfortably to accept
its one passenger

After a quick dive into the temple
to say hello to the forest goddess
I walk back to the house

A few vendors are out with carts —
bananas, green and yellow, mangoes and
Kashmir apples   a temple bell rings

then another   crows caw in the wake of sound
stores are shuttered   locks in place

Neighborhood ghosts hang around
an empty vending stand with its sign
Fast Food and a menu scribbled in Malayalam

A distant hum of a motor starting   a boat
beginning to slice the backwaters

CRAYONS

My young son brings home a sticky red chalk
he calls a crayon. Soon mangos glare
from his pencil drawing, and red brick of houses.

The next day he exchanges with a classmate,
the red one for a green to attach leaves onto the mangos
and paint windows on the houses.

By the end of the week his picture is complete
with black birds winging through a blue sky,
gray stick people entering and exiting the houses
shaded by an orchard, a bright yellow sun
descending into the turquoise strip of Arabian Sea.

He dreams of his picture all night,
in the morning the colors have exploded
their frame, spilled onto the walls of our room.

He wants me to promise his own box of crayons,
so he can shelter under their magical hues.

Diary Entry, 1940

Gandhiji came to Alleppey yesterday. His words
make me want to march with him all the way to the
northern cities: Surat, Allahabad, Dandi. Each time
he calls for independence and swaraj, I say, *yes, I
want that too, right here, in my home.* I shout with the
crowd, *Zindabad,* and lift my fist up high along with
a thousand other fists. Cousin Kichu also shouts
passionately, sweat dotting his forehead. Husband
refused to come to this rally. He says Gandhi is
destroying the country. The British are good for us
lazy people. They have what Indians do not have,
punctuality, order, cleanliness. I don't agree. If you
look at my kitchen, you will see it is clean and the
vessels are in order, and I wake up every day at the
same time, bathe before anyone, serve food to the
family on time; even the cows know when it is time
for them to be milked; the crows come for morsels
to the back door at the same time each afternoon
as if they have clocks in their bellies. Husband
asks what's so great about the mahatma. He says,
Churchill's right to call Gandhiji the half-naked fakir.
Our great sages wore loin cloths, some not even that,
but clothes do not mark one's greatness, but I dare
not tell him that, especially when he is in his tailored
suit ready to go to work. I want to ask him, why
are people following the half-naked man and not
you dressed in your London best? He'll simply say
they are ignorant fools and I am a foolish wife to get
excited about rallies to oust our benevolent British.
It's startling that I can think of the mahatma's
struggle when I'm low.

WHAT EAST INDIA COMPANY SHIPS CARRIED

Silk, cotton, cardamom, cloves,
indigo, cumin, ginger, tea,
opium, cinnamon, Sanskrit, gold,
diamonds, coral, coffee, steel,

hookahs, paintings, elephants, deeds,
maps, rails, engines, slaves,
dictionaries, brains, poems, briefs,
dust, roaches, charms, laws,

pariah, juggernaut, nautch-girl, coolie,
monkeys, aluminum, small pox, rum,
rebellion, Gandhi, copper, wheat,
hemp, jute, newspapers, gum,

rubber, sugar, bricks, gods,
thrones, sutras, blueprints, rats,
sitar, leather, ivory, wood,
mahogany, monsoon, muslin.

JOKE

He is so beautifully bad   my boy
I watch him grow   I laugh
at his silliness   yesterday he picked up
my older daughter-in-law's silver
beetle-nut box   she had turned to stir
the soup
he slipped it under the mat

she looked everywhere   when she asked me
I kept a straight face   Ambi was behind her
putting his finger to his lips

as in the prayers and the epics
his petal-lips were pursed

have you seen it   where could it have gone
while she was upstairs looking for her lost
treasure   his laughter burst
downstairs   he is so beautifully bad

SITALA RESPONDS TO THE PHOTOGRAPHER

Mr. Photographer bending under the hood of your camera
Clicking, cranking the lever, your clicks and cranks vex
Me. You're one-eyed Kabandha, roving among ephemera

To capture a scene that holds, if not any aura,
At least a mundane truth. Are you sure you can affix
My passing smile? Under the hood of your camera,

Your singular response is to click away through a plethora
Of emotions: Husband's eyes that could jinx
Anything good, the kids, mere ephemera

As they sit at our feet like budding fauna,
An unsmiling wife who does not mix
Pleasure with staring at the veil of your camera.

My baby I am holding like a ball, extra
Tight, is about to scream. Are you done with this house of sticks,
This almost-permanence among all the ephemera?

Don't look at me, I speak without drama.
To shoot husband and kids you don't need any tricks,
Mr. Photographer bending under the roof of your camera,
Peering into your lens to capture mere ephemera.

The Kitchen Years

my day stretches like the river
pots and pans are rocks
I could be a mermaid stretched among them
or I could be moss
a crow shaking off dew . . .

I see the lone papaya among the leaves
a sliver of sunbeam cutting through them
flooding the grass

could the goddess of song sail across the room
in the smoke hanging like gossamer mist
among the black ceiling and walls

see me framed by my dripping hair knotted loosely
as I sit fanning the flames
and plant a song on my tongue?

I am a drying bed among coconut fiber and soap
wanting to be saturated by flow of syllable and syntax
away from these yawning steel mouths
the moist crushing dark

Naming in the Era of Independence

Son, don't let my grand-daughter carry my name,
my past, religion, duty, customs, tribe, line,
deaden her heart, play someone else's game,

freeze the songs even flies in filth are free to hum.
It won't be my name she'll have to sign.
Son, don't let my grand-daughter carry my name.

Say instead, she'll be one the wind proclaims;
imagine how softly they brush your mind,
the light syllables inviting people to play a game.

Your tongue longs to call out, love, *Prem*,
roll out the rest, so people say, *What a find!*
It's good your grand-daughter doesn't carry your name.

Why make her like the sad wife of Ram?
Make new. Cast your net wide.
Why play the same old game?

Her modern name, to some a shame,
to others, not new enough, but a blind
detour around my name.
Hush! Let her invent a new game.

TRYST WITH DEATH

— *"Storm on the Ganges, with Mrs. Hastings near the
Col-gon Rocks," by William Hodges. Oil on Canvas.* 1790

I am she.
I am also the boat. I have drunk that spray.
I have seen those evil rocks.

I visited death's brink,
seen its shimmering eyes in the suffocating spray,
choked and twisted in the heave and dive

of an angry river goddess
churning out enough passion to oust the Governor's lady.
I know people speak of her with awe,

"What a brave woman
to go off on a tourist boat without husband
or friend, and that, too, on the unpredictable Ganga!"

Little do they know an abnormal silence
rises around me in 1940, as I sit in this hall
at noon gazing at the storm in this painting,

Mrs. Hastings' white gown and skin my own,
her terror my barometric needle
marking fear balling up in my belly

as if Ganga is throwing *my* door open
and rushing in, her current unstoppable. I beat my arms,
throw sheets, pillows, pots, pans and rags to divert

                    the onslaught
and swim frantically to feel the shifting moss
under my toes, edge my way onto firmer ground.

        Oh, she must've been doomed to recall
that precipice, the falling back, that teetering —
Hodges, did you grasp that, too,

            as you twisted cerulean blue onto the canvas,
know the void in her belly, England fading,
unlike the husband who had India on his mind?

        Engulfed by rising waves in my home,
I can hear her plea, "Warren, had you been there with me,
you would now quit and go home,

            to lie in a hammock under a mild English sun,
relieved, and in days we'll only remember
the spectacular double rainbow on the waters."

Karma Blues

Can I recover the song I dreamed at dawn?
The cock's shrill crowing scattered the notes
I held together with all my strength.
Mist fills the hollow where the song dwelled.

The cock's shrill crowing shattered the notes
Like love silenced by a train whistle.
Mist fills the hollow where the song dwelled
Thickening as the hours pass.

Like love silenced by a train whistle,
His slap among the jollity of the wedding hall
Stinging me, tightening my throat as the hours pass.
I withdraw into my tent of shame.

His slap among the jollity of the wedding hall
Punched a hole into my kindness.
I withdraw into my tent of shame
Each time his hand and my shock flash before me.

He has punched a hole into my kindness.
How can I forgive him my public humiliation?
Each time his hand and my shock flash before me,
Anger's salt makes my wound raw.

How can I forgive him my public humiliation,
Especially when he is not conscious of his crime?
Anger's salt makes my wound raw.
I pray time will grow its scab to protect me.

Men, you say, are not conscious of the crime
They do to women. I know he will pay
In time when I grow a scab to protect me.
It is time for me to sing to exorcise me of him.

If you hit a woman, you will pay
Through your sons and grandsons.
It is time for me to sing to exorcise me
Of his evil, an incubus worming into me.

One's sins continue in our sons and grandsons;
This is the law of karma. Was he blind
To his evil, an incubus, worming into me?
I need to use cunning in the face of karma,
A magician's shawl for the song of my being.

YOGURT

Before going to bed, I enter the kitchen lit
by flickering lamps, bring milk to a boil, pour it
into a clay pot and let it cool, do the finger test,
spoon sour yogurt into it with a vigorous stir.

The pot sits all night on the toasty hearth, listening to scuttles
and whispers of bugs, until they disappear with the first slab
of light falling across the floor through the porthole-like window.

Entering the kitchen, I first head to the pot,
open it to admire the thick yogurt, its creamy, porous skin,
before putting it away in a cool place. At lunch, I serve
icy slices of it, along with fluffy rice and lemon pickle moons.

Noon

My Husband Is Ruled by Proverbs

Know how they rule us?
Punk-choo-al, that's what they are,
so if you know my car arrives at 9
then you need to serve my food
by 8:41, have my shoes polished
by 8:55, so I am ready.

Get the place cleaned up today,
why wait until tomorrow,   ˋ
for procrastination is the thief of time;
how do you think you got your big
house, a car and servants?
My boss sees I don't waste a minute
and am a genius at solving his
Schylla-and-Charibdes problems;
when he smiles I smell the bonus
right away. You can't make hay
if you chat with that cousin
always caught in the horns of a dilemma,
about career, clothes, or radio programs.

Keep away from useless neighbors pointing their fingers
at me; they should know
people in glass houses should not throw stones.
Make a list of things to do, don't whine
for a stitch in time saves nine,
and stop asking for new saris or hoping
for relatives to visit us,
as I have said many times, if wishes were
horses beggars would ride.

I will take you and the children to Tiruchi
during the holidays when my boss will
be vacationing at a hill station.
He has taught me all work and no play
makes Jack a dull boy.

GRANDFATHER CLOCK

Tick-tock-tick-tock, it ticks into my brain.
Its quick-quick, ready-set-go-I-mean-business
frightens me awake, as if a train
were screaming into my consciousness
that I must catch before it pulls out. *Aiyo*,
I can't stand its clang-clang.

Is this Victoria's summer bungalow,
your office, or Yama's haunt?
You say this clock makes our home modern,
but don't you see behind this behemoth
a zoo of spiders, lizards, roaches and a fan
of cobwebs? It's an old man with bad breath.

Please get this annoyance out of our house
even if the world dismisses my grouse.

OBLITERATION

When I stayed in a room darkened with bed sheets
for fear of exposing my fetus to the darkness eating the sun
chewing it bit by bit and then plunging the earth in pitch dark

and the son in my womb

you moved between him and me   your largeness
eclipsing his littleness

my protective rays growing dim despite the curtains
my fingers resting lightly on my spherical dome
listening to the tiny breath beating its soft drum

your drone stifling him
achieving what the sun could not.

UNMASKED

Husband's face among the Kathakali dancers:
what could he be doing wandering into the *Mahabharatha?*
I know them all, Bhima, Draupadi, Duryodhana,[2]

not this stranger, unmasked, unpainted,
trotting to and fro like a blind bull
among the powerful. Does he hope to band
with Duryodhana and unleash some plot?

Get away, I hiss, not wanting to disturb
the enraptured audience
sitting on moonlit grass.

Why is he smirking as Draupadi's sari
is pulled, yards of it, in the grand hall?
Shame on you, I want to yell,

but my throat is stuck.
Does the audience think he is part of the action?

---

2. In the *Mahabharatha,* Duryodhana, the oldest of the Kaurava
cousins, humiliates Draupadi, the wife of the Pandavas, when
Yuddhistira, the oldest of the Pandava brothers, loses everything to
the Kauravas in a game of dice. Because of her devotion to Krishna,
Draupadi's disrobing, ordered by Duryodhana, can never be
completed because her sari becomes miraculously infinite, keeping her
covered.

Next is the war scene, and there is Husband
between Karna and Kunti.[3] I rage,
smelling betrayal. I mouth soundlessly,
Let Kunti bless her son even if he turns away.

Get away from him.
Husband does not hear me, he whispers into Karna's ear.
Does he think he is talking to his son, Ambi?

Drums roll. Flames leap.
Mother and son part like the river.

---

3. Kunti, the mother of the Pandava brothers, has a child by the sun
god, when she is an unmarried teenager. She places this child in a
boat and sets it afloat. The child is found by a cowherd and is brought
up as Karna and is later befriended by Duryodhana. Kunti, much
later, discloses to Karna his birth story, hoping he would side with his
Pandava brothers, but he stands steadfastly by Duryodhana and the
Kauravas.

THE CHATTERBOX

Husband's gone to his office,
so I walk to Cousin Kichu's, relax on a stool
in the hall, Kichu in his armchair.
We jabber about the kids,
oldest daughter-in-law's travails
with her husband, his sudden
vanishings some nights,
who I met at the temple,
what's cooking in the pot,
my youngest son's exploits.

I ask him about our old friends,
and on and on into the quiet heat,
as if we've not talked in years
when we'd seen each other
only a couple of days before.

I am back in my childhood,
laughing, throwing up my legs,
my sari a puddle around my shins,
hair disheveled despite the oil
to calm it down, my tongue racing
to capture my life...

Kichu listens, laughs with abandon,
feeds me bananas, jackfruit wedges,
gluey leftovers from a pan,
and I eat his offering between
sentences. I know he worries
about his boys, his girl's dowry,
but his forehead is clear of lines.

"It's four," he says, glancing at the clock,
  and in answer it clangs four times.
  Kichu knows my woes, does not ask
  about the bruises, we don't find
  words for my pain.

  It's nice to be children again,
  be on the same team.
  We chat all the way to the door,
  and part with, "I'll visit after the festival
  if I can." Kichu nods, ties his veshti
  tighter around his waist, knowing
"if I can" is a formality meant
  for nosy neighbors.

Dumb Faith

Will astrological
charts, superstitions, rituals,
endless prostrations before
stone idols
guard our tenuous life?

Do turtles, crows, worms
pray for rescue
from their eat-and-be eaten world?

Are trees indifferent to a higher
being because they cannot speak
and walk, or because they know
that ask-and-you-shall- receive
human belief is, sadly,
human?

But I cloud pain with illusion.
I plead, I cry,
but the gods are quiet,
they've quit their marble and granite
forms. I want to curse,
call out their indifference,
but I tell myself
they must be at
obnoxiously loud parties;

if they were to hear me and the turtles,
crows, worms and trees,
they would break with an
overdose of emotion.

Oiled Hinges

Pick up the wash, shake out each garment,
hang it on the line.

Lift each dried plate, cup, bowl,
place them neatly on the shelf.

Put away notebooks and pencils lying
on the floor, roll the mats, dust and mop.
All is clean, you say

as if this will wipe memory:

the temple dancer's dark fingers
around his hips, his fair form pressing
her down, her full lips.

I am the ravaged wife standing by the door.

MISTRESS

I think she's pretty, this temple dancer
although I see her at a distance,
recognize her from her hair combed high
so it falls bouncy and seductive
grabbed by a string of jasmine.
Cousin Kichu points her out,
"Look," and his eyes shoot
toward the spot under a flaring
tamarind by the temple.

The dancer and my son stand together,
their forms dim in twilight.
"She's pretty," I say. Her gold bangles,
necklace, nose ring, earrings,
anklets jangle me

as do her hips' wildness
held by a sober sari
and a gold waist belt.
"Let's go home," I shake Kichu
from his trance.
"She is beautiful," he murmurs.

Dark like the moon's shadow,
all that brightness just about to burst
forth, I think, a sucker for beauty,
forgetting I hated her.
Why steal my son, why
make him forget his wife,
his family,
why?

I know this momentary madness;
I feel its power when I sing,
or a line of poetry forms in my head
like larva ballooning.
I know his letting go of rules,

that trance, amnesia of place,
house, earth, sky,
when she moves under him
and draws him deeper into her coming.

Sex

shuffling by my side
strange hands spreading my thighs

tearing my sari
setting it afloat over my face

darkness

his large rock growing in me
shakes me
then shakes me off

sweat in my nostrils
blood on my lips

darkness

nine months later
a wail in my lap

I only own
the yearning in my breasts

DIARY ENTRY, 1930

Yesterday something strange happened. Ambi
was running in the yard holding an imaginary
rifle, screaming *Doo-doo-thuppakki, police-kaaran
pondaati*. It is funny, but how does he know what
a rifle looks like, what it does, how it sounds, how
to hold it? He's never seen one. Unless he has been
looking at the newspapers his father reads and has
seen pictures of British soldiers with guns. I know
war is on in Europe and the East Indies—radio
broadcasts, news reels before movies at the local
Lotus Cinema we have been to a couple of times
with Ambi are filled with the smells and sounds of
war—but Ambi's world is just school and cricket
and pranks. Our police only carry sticks, not guns,
and they are hardly seen in our neighborhood except
when they come during Diwali for gifts. A sad lot,
most of them, really, and their pay is so bad, they
look hungry, barely able to defend themselves, let
alone us. That stupid rhyme, I know, it's nonsense,
lots of kids sing it, but it makes me shiver. I tried
pulling that imaginary rifle from him and he chased
me with it screaming that rhyme: *I am the innocent
wife shot by my policeman husband.*

LETTER TO SAROJINI

The things I love in your poems:
nightingales, peacocks, bangle sellers, bangles.
I have yet to see a nightingale here in my corner of Kerala.
There is a peacock in the temple but it does not dance,
the bangle sellers are morose and show the same dull colors.
If only they captured the hues of spring!

I sing of nature too—nothing exotic, only cows,
dung, household chores, occasionally flowers,
their wicks lit by woe and snuffed by it.
I, too, hear the cries of vendors, am lured
by snake charmers, and seduced by royalty.

Love pulses in your lines but the rhythms and the rhymes
so sweet, sweet, hide too much like purdah.
I, too, get tempted to escape into my lines,
visit a glorious past even if it may only seem so
from this distance, lift the veil off the faces
of beautiful begums, peek into their love
letters, describe lovers in the classical style.

Why don't you write about our struggle in our homes,
our country ruled by whites who don't understand our lives,
your feelings about Gandhiji, your friends, your favorite haunts,
your house, your family? Are you happy, sad, excited
at the urgency you see in the papers of more arrests,
more marches, more unjust laws, more terror?

Why no mention of our salt, the jangle of our chains,
odors of dark spaces, prisons, sweat, crowds,
cramped hearts and cities, blood on walls,
in speeches, in mothers' cries? These too can seduce.

A PARTICULAR SHAPE

Four children and two
miscarriages came quickly.
My mind checked out.
I was only my body
receiving   giving.

A well in my heart

at the bottom of it
my mind snipped off.

Then   Ambi like a poem.
Will he remain pure outside my reach?
The pale sun shines,
its silver reaches me
and I find the bottom rung.

✳

Ambi's dreams are large.
They began when the cord was cut
and grew larger than Husband's
British company, larger now than India
and Pakistan.

I write to him   your brother did this
your sister said that
but he writes about his climb
and this warms me
makes everything bearable.

*

What could the father do but sulk
as the son waved goodbye
from the dusty train window?

No smile or cheer.
Yet my heart was light.

BOY-MAN

Five-sons-three-daughters rich, I still feel bereft.
Without clutching Ambi's crisp shirt to my face,
hearing him hold a tune, loss digs deep.

He doesn't let his tears show, he's being a man.
I need to get a degree, get a job, settle down,
he says gruffly, tasting his newly cracked voice.

Trains will whisk him to Trivandrum, Bombay,
Karachi, to be free of my love, his father's downturned
lip, the bunk's lurch his lullaby, my flickering dark.

Goodbye dear one, you will be a fine man,
test the worth of caring like biting into coins.
Flipping bread and calendars will teach me to wait

for a scrawled yellow postcard, a telegram stitched
to gauze, an omen from the forest goddess foretelling
your wedding, later starched napkins and Dettol.

POSTCARD FROM KABUL, 1956

Everything here—
mountains, ponds, women
drinks, hair, roads, houses

teeth, love, hospitality
wind, men, dawn, night
trees, markets, Quran, fruit—

is the color of
almonds.

FORT COCHIN

high walls
behind them
a beating sea

trees gone wild
the road stilled
by wind-dazed stone

walk all the way down
around the curve
and still further
to the jetty
by colonial houses

nothing's buffeted
except anchored skiffs
and patience of workers
waiting for boats
to ferry them home

birds have quit the trees
they are dancing on invisible
wings of winds
how they join and split apart

even their scattering is not random
bougainvillea and hibiscus
have learned to simply be

not easy with all this whistling
and above the swaying world
a drunken brawl

Evening

THE ART OF THE INVISIBLE

I know what it is like to be invisible,
the rolled-up mat in the corner,
its design of a blue dancing peacock hidden
in the commonplace tan tassels and weave,
fresh scent of day now here, now lost in the stench
of fish rising as fishermen plied the river.

When each day commands me awake to a river
of children and chores, I don an invisible
cloak to flow through the hours, so the stench
of feelings will not subdue me at every corner
as I brush and cut, wash, dust and weave,
knowing with each step that art is indeed hidden.

Think of how the perfect pebble remains hidden
until you stumble upon it by the river,
or you discover the secret rose in the weave
that the carpet maker tried to keep invisible.
Like spite or love, death or life round the corner
is passive until it roils you with its scent or stench.

Songs within me lift me above the stench
of household politics, the angry patriarchs hidden
and waiting to bound out of every corner
feeding their darkness to the goddess by the river.
But the goddess who keeps herself invisible,
said in a dream, "Let me hear the ragas you weave."

I now linger longer over the rhymes weaving
through a song as fishermen stay with the stench
of fish though twilight casts trees into invisibility.
My daughters argue over treasures hidden
until my husband's last rites are performed by the river.
Now gold, copper and brass spring in every corner.

To my youngest daughter-in-law standing in the corner
frightened by the raised voices weaving
their way through the streets to the river,
I say, "Stay like the lotus above the stench.
There may be something you value still hidden
marking its place among the invisible."

Thus my life turns a corner: From beneath my weave of pleats,
I lift an ancient vessel masked with river stench,
"Cook your songs in this; they'll sizzle out of invisibility."

Boat Song

tha thi thi thai thom thom thom
tha thi thi thai thom thom thom

there were two boys who loved to row
they ate, loved, breathed ocean song
day and night they pumped their arms
until like crests their biceps rose

tha thi thi thai thom thom thom
tha thi thi thai thom thom thom

they became men and still they rowed
so smitten were they with the sound of the sea
when mother asked them to select a bride
they said, *find us wives of ocean hue*

tha thi thi thai thom thom thom
tha thi thi thai thom thom thom

mother searched high and low for women
the colors of turquoise, gray, and blue
but she could only find girls who were tan
for that is the race that peoples this land

tha thi thi thai thom thom thom
tha thi thi thai thom thom thom

the boys looked at the brown and burnt faces
and off they went to the sea to row
so they could see in the water's gaze
their soul mate, friend, and lover true

tha thi thi thai thom thom thom
tha thi thi thai thom thom thom

from one long voyage they returned
to rapid percussion on the shore
they saw their mother wearing a frown
that her matchmaking efforts were in vain

tha thi thi thai thom thom thom
tha thi thi thai thom thom thom

mother, you have tried to see the ocean
mirrored on women's skins,
girth, hair, walk, and eyes,
but you have forgotten a vital place.

tha thi thi thai thom thom thom
tha thi thi thai thom thom thom

what is that? asked the mother
the heart, dear mother, is like the sea,
colorless, knows the highs and the lows,
the shallows and depths, sand and rock.

tha thi thi thai thom thom thom
tha thi thi thai thom thom thom

there were two girls who dreamed of waves,
grew up gentle with salt in their hair,
their hearts were little fists of wonder
that rose and fell to the beat of the sea.

tha thi thi thai thom thom thom
tha thi thi thai thom thom thom

the brides looked bright on their wedding day,
by evening they turned brown, by night
they were dark, their hearts so open
the sea laughed, the boats danced and danced.

tha thi thi thai thom thom thom
tha thi thi thai thom thom thom

even today on summer nights
you hear the two men and their wives
hum tunes salted with life's tangles
and lovers bear their agony a little longer.

Paean to Saraswati

1

Saraswati has made my tongue her bed of thorns.
I shoot dirty limericks, twist my tongue like schoolgirls,
into a snake, a rose, a cup, roll it as if to swallow it.
It writhes like a snake charmer's pet that wants to curl
back into the basket, tired of the song he pipes.
Aadu paambe vilayadu paambe. Over and over.
My venom keeps my audience distant, dazed.

2

Speech is a woman with flowing tresses covering
her ample curves. She floats in air sparking the current
among us. Our flesh desires her flesh to keep us warm
with the energy that keeps us human. When she reclines
on paper, we are overcome by her infinite geometries,
her charged outpourings.

3

Let Saraswati place a drop of honey on my tongue
so I begin again, see the mist clear above
the backwaters, boats leaning on the shore,
trees bearing down like pregnant women,
smear of sunshine like turmeric glowing on skin.

Let Saraswati carve a path for me to walk in her
word gardens, snake gods lifting their wry faces
in anticipation; let her place her swan feather
in my hand and bid me write so she can abandon
her bed of thorns. She carries pain for me gladly,
has so much light that she can pour a little
into my dark conniving soul, so ready to wed suicide.

Dung Song

I don't want to sing about betrayal
or treachery, Husband glaring at me
as I turn away from a gale of laughter,
or cold gripping my heart, the slap
I don't see coming, faces spinning.

I don't want to sing about the pity
of many eyes, the pain, my shame,
shriller than the pipes screaming their music
when bride and groom exchange
garlands heavy with rose scent,
salt in my mouth spurning
the syrupy halwa with its cardamom sting,

the satisfaction in the wad of betel leaf
tucked into every right cheek after the wedding
and children like butterflies flitting among guests.
I don't want to sing about any of this,

or about the wedded pair leaving the pandol
as strangers, or of Husband calling me, Sitala,
come here, fetch this. I am going to sing
about the product of Krishna's favorite beast,
I will sing about cow dung.

Cow Dung Cakes

"Her cow dung song was hilarious"
— *Sitala's youngest daughter-in-law*

Cow dung dark and damp like rainy night
lying in little hills in fields

on the path to the river temple post office
the mister's office building

I pat each scoop into round patties
like henna cooling my skin orange

under mid-day sun they dry
around me   their queen
into asteroids and planets

drawing sacrificial fire
to their fragrance

they fuel the stove on which I
make sweet tea fit for the gods

what is merely dung to you is to me
beauty   dear friend

the stench lies in my home
not in these rich brown cakes

ODE TO THE DECEMBER FLOWER

Lilac tracing paper cut into small petals
bunched together in layers,
you like to show yourself off
on women's hair, strung around a bun
or twisted around a braid,

or if you have nowhere to go,
you spread yourself on the sidewalk,
on the front porch,
or patiently wait on the tree
your color deepening among the green
and against the slow rise of winter light.

When do you disappear, where to,
without a trace? Women wait like
demented lovers for months,
unable to utter your name,
since you never revealed it,

until one day you spot them
with your lilac gaze, and they suddenly
look up, as they catch your scentless
shadow.

LIST

rice
lentils
flour
jackfruit
jaggery
peppermint
notebook
write welcome song
buy Malayalam newspaper
get new calendar
go to dispensary
Tipu's coffee
coir rope
ready pickle jars
make budget
make up expense list
practice old songs
write new song
create new flower kolam
pay papadum lady
ask Kichu to send telegram to Ambi
tell priest puja is canceled
tell Gopalan to book tickets
DDT for pests

Indigo

Tear this room open,
you will hear agony and flight,
smell the stale odor of sex, dank clothes
on the line that have seen fierce monsoon.

Pierce the center of this house with a sword.
Your blade will pass air thick with cooking
smoke, sandalwood and myrrh,
before it sticks into a vermilion floor.

Tear my heart open and you will turn blue
with the assault of hoarded thought blackening
arteries in its wild, storm-ravaged muscle.
You will pine

for the delicate scent of skin
you want your tongue to astonish.

ONAM

            Soak the rice, drain the water,
dry the grains, grind them into powder, prepare jaggery syrup
on a hot stove, and keep stirring till you can stick your finger in,

            lift it, see the glue separating
in thin lines as you un-stick thumb and index finger, working against
their pull toward each other, their kiss and release, a signal to blend

            the rice flour into the boiling syrup,
throw in fried teeth of coconut and coarsely ground cardamom,
both meant to make joy last on the fickle tongue.

            This is *kali* heralding a new year,
sticky-sweet carbohydrate celebrating energy of earth and body,
kali, with its short vowel sound that marks its difference
from the dark,

            dancing goddess, the word that flits
between food and play, both filling us with pleasure, the right word,
the right game for the soul in the festival of grain.

MY BODY DOES NOT GIVE UP

I know some pleasures:
Chiku juice flowing down
my fingers to my elbow as my teeth sink
into the brown pulp

I swallow its nectar

thrill of water tickling my soles
coolness riding up my calves
wetness seeping into my heart

song rising from the pit of my
belly to my throat

released, how it wings upward like a bird
my voice teasing me and me teasing my voice
silk against my skin

my child drinking his fill

so softly he holds my nipple
his suck turning me inside out
a fullness and emptiness   of seeing

and not seeing

all this despite living with a stone husband.

Margaret Sanger in India

— based on Helen Keller's letter to Margaret Sanger, Dec. 8, 1952

I got off the steamer in Bombay, the heat
beating down on us as we rowed to the docks.

Salty air, smoke from peanut carts
acrid dust from motor cars, a heaving sea.

Oh, the heady colors — from jasmine like snow
on women's raven hair to ballooning shawls.

Planned Parenthood Association is launched in India,
despite the Comstock Law and imprisonment.

You've said it, dear, along with President Nehru
and Lady Rama Rau, we are the triumvirate.

Soon people will be enlightened about birth control
so each child will be clothed and fed, fulfilling

women's work as creator-caretaker. Getting folks
to see its importance is far from Herculean

in India where there's no religious prohibition
on birth control, no Christians knocking

down my door with death threats, police blackmailing me,
my husband forced to become my armor.

Nehru greeted me with roses, and the other day
a silk shawl was draped around my shoulders,

a traditional honor for important guests. My words here,
no different from those in New York, are revered.

I am seen as luminous by all who have worked
ardently for Independence. Why can't our country

see freedom of nation and freedom of women
to plan their family in the same light?

My Promethean task is chaff in this wind.

WHY I COULD NOT PLAN MY FAMILY, 1960

Everyone these days talks about family planning,
not just in Bombay where my younger son lives,
but even in this corner of Kerala, so far from Delhi.

What we women thought in our heads privately
as we ranted to our friends that we were pregnant
again and laughed self-consciously for it meant

we were having sex and our husbands were still randy
at their age when the grandchildren were appearing,
all our code words for sex became public
as the government announced,

Two is plenty, which means I'll have fewer grandchildren,
let me see, a mere 2 or 3 from each child, totaling 15–20
rather than 40–45, still, enough for a family feast.

I'm glad my daughters won't have the burdens I bore,
they'll have time to enjoy comforts with their
husbands, of course, if the husbands have sense
to enjoy them than waste time in quarrels and stupidities.

Anyway, who wants to hear an old woman's rants?
All I want to say is I'm glad my daughters can visit doctors
to get advice about when to have babies and how many

instead of getting pregnant and trying to drink vile
cocktails produced by the local quack to get rid of
the *thing*, or following old timers' tales
of the sour cud's power to begin your period—

you sit under the tamarind tree in the yard
chewing piles of tamarind until your body rebels,
and you swear off the sour fruit.

All this in secret, for we learned the art of secrecy
about sex, snacks, shopping, and with it came
the terrible wait of discovery: did the thing work

and were we free until the next time the husband got hot,
or do we have to carry again mournfully, fate-humbled?
How we gambled with our lives
and went about chores with a vengeance!

Midnight

SINGLE, 1947

I laugh when no one's looking.
I can sing again.
They don't know I'm finally free.

They thought they had stripped me of my womanhood,
shaved all my hair off,
wrapped me like a pear in a brown sari,

no blouse, my breasts dangling.
As if I was ever tied to these jewels
or my dot.

They rubbed the dot on my forehead,
it must look like a raging sunset.
The funeral was yesterday.

They came and pulled my bangles off—
Earrings, nose ring, toe ring,
mangalasutra. If they had pulled at my tongue,

I would have bitten them raw.

A widow.
I'm free.
India is also free.

Youthful Evening

1

I love walking around Bhagavati temple,
my bare feet sinking into the cool sand.
It is hot, but I don't care as I circumambulate
the shrine three times, my feet in heaven.

The peacocks are strutting about, spreading
their blue-green feathers. Perhaps it will rain.
They are dancing expecting dense, moist leaves
to drip, drip, drip as they glow wild in loud air.

A song rises within me in raga Vasantha,
spring meter of rejuvenation. My feathers flare.
I walk with a light step, my baldness, my widowhood,
my age, my brown sari,
my lack of jewelry or husband forgotten.

2

Men and women roll on the stone floor,
round and round they circle the sanctum,
their bodies cranked by some alien will.
Penance makes me dizzy.

My heart is with the carefree peacocks,
the heady incense, the divine sweetness
of rice pudding I eat from a tiny slice
of yellow-green banana leaf.

So much joy wherever I turn,
as when Husband took me to Humayun's Tomb
in Delhi. Peacocks among the dancing leaves
guarded the spirits of princesses and begums
moving around the mausoleum. My dream disrupted
with his order, *Stop dawdling, walk fast.*

Beyond the pirouetting birds
the shadow of another world.

A Meditation on Rain in Ragam Mohanam

Gulmohar trees sigh
on lawns filled with pools of cloud,
gray sky wrings its last drops.

Ga Pa Da Pa Da Sa

Late summer plants are dervishes,
their robes wild

Ga Pa Da Pa Da Pa   Ga Pa Da Pa Da Pa   Pa Da Sa, Pa Da Sa,
Sa Da Ga . . .

Wind and rain sweep through me
I am sparkling dew,
the shine after rain or sleep

Ga Ri Ga . . . Ga . . . Ga . . . Pa Sa
Ga Pa Da Pa Da Sa Sa Ri Ga

I am air on your tongue
your very breath

Sa Da Pa Ga Ri, Ga Pa Ri, Sa Da Sa.

AFTER THE FUNERAL

I don't remember the funeral.
I mourn the numb heart.
Dumb fart!

Women sang a dirge.
Dry-eyed, I listened to their *oppari*.
Hired pity!

Husband gone,
gods stand next in line.
Hang devotion!

Thirteen days of rites
to help him land in paradise.
Fat prize!

Counting steps room to room
counting moons.
Spin, loom, spin . . . or
I'll swoon from boredom.

Ten years from now I'll still be
too young to die.
Come, magic spirits,
at least I won't live a lie.

DIARY ENTRY, 1948

I have stopped doing puja, reciting endless slokas,
performing rituals. No one notices. I merge into the
dark corners of the house, since I am never expected
anymore in the main rooms cooking or cleaning. Not
expected to perform puja is a new freedom. Now I
can use the time, when I am not watering the plants
or doing odd jobs, to dream up songs even if I don't
sing them, imagine the path of a raga. This is like
prayer, an invisible spire of smoke rising from my
belly. These Sanskrit slokas are like bees buzzing
in my mouth. I want to spit them out and relish the
beatitude of a dry mouth, soft tongue and quiet ears.
I don't torment myself with them anymore. Instead,
I disappear to the backyard where the outhouses are
and rest under a jacaranda when others are rattling
off their orations. Listen to this Tamil song by
Bharatiyar[4] like butter on my tongue. When I sing
it, even my body feels supple. Yesterday I sang it
to the daughters-in-law and my daughters lounging
on their straw mats after lunch. Their smiles lit the
room. The men in the other room fell silent.

---

4. Tamil nationalist poet and freedom fighter

Wild Syllables

rivers   rain   birds   sky
    fishermen   waters   wild
                                                     catch

f l o o d g a t e s   surge

        hunger   mad

           catamarans

dip   climb
  and   dive

                                void dark
        birds   spin   heart   dim

boats   drown
               wild   catch

drrrummm   rain   barrel   glut

  gutter   brim   overflow   roar   drrrummm

    refuge   gnash   turbulence   blaze

ship   stone   slate   slab
    empty shore   debris   grate

feathers   scum   bark   trough
  moan   silence   cede

    quiet

lift   sun   watery   brief

j a g g e d c o a s t   endear   fish

             clearing   spirits   Sing
blue   sing blue   flesh   land
    sing blue   sing blue

LETTER TO MY DAUGHTER-IN-LAW

From the grace of your walk,
the way you offer me dinner,
roll out a mat for me to sit,
I know you will be good to my son,
tender to your kids,
but I cannot predict if you will suffer.

Even these walls speak my history,
the trees whisper my grief. My tears
have drenched him in my womb
and he grew up wading in it
though I placed stepping stones,
smooth and dry for his foothold.

But how to protect my son from
the sudden arc of a hand killing
the air, cannon fire of words,
then a minefield alive years
after the battle? Will he step
onto safe land with your help,
build and carry, draw silk
from your hands, learn how to
seek succor his father failed at?

Daughter-in-law, notice,
I don't order you about, but revel
in my son's fortune. I pray
he will know how to keep you
walking gracefully.

Dawn

The Karmic Cycle

He stands talking, one moment a ghost,
clothes hanging loosely on his frame,
head floating above white cotton,

the next moment the laughing young man
full of handsome vigor,
sparkling smile mirroring mine,

three decades vanish and I am the little girl
looking up taking instruction how to, what to,
when to, looking now through the scrim

of sudden air between me sitting down,
he standing tall despite the illness
and the heart's timid beat:

He followed his parents' instruction,
so well—until he now asks,

"Why does this emotion steal into me, this anger,
a cobra that rears as if I don't exist,
then vanishes before I can kill it? Why,

where, how? I can't understand it, I can't,"
his words echoing among paddy and palm,
"I can't, where does it come from?"

✳

Where does it come from,
this emotion that twists in the gut,
forces my fingers into fists?

I could jab a hole into any object
but I always aim at the fragile—
a kick that stifles, a bomb.

I don't heed the warning of the wise:
Kopum, root of self-destruction
no holiness can redeem.

*

No amount of ritual can redeem
his rage hurricaning me through our eleven children,
some dead, some alive.

I see my sons transform in the gloom.
The gods keeping watch, wearily
shut their eyes. Darkness closes in.

There is no letting up. Imagine
if the *Ramayana* was only strife
with no unions. My sons are now

the hands and lips of my husband.
They can't translate tenderness
even if their brain thinks it.

They carry English on their tongue
mastery of order, the master's whip,
their instincts marooned.

The river asks for fishermen,
wives wake up to the mahatma,
the country is aglow with revolution.

But my handsome sons have
not worked with clay.
They mold sons in their image.

*

Soon after Independence, they mold sons:
Relatives say, *he looks like his father,*
a replica of his grandfather.

The thing is, the apple does not fall
far from the tree: My sons like to
declaim in English proverbs

more than reciting the Vedas.
The ancients knew the way,
they understood emotion,

how to claim it and calm it.
Had my sons been scientists
they would have searched.

Or even if blinded by faith,
they would've circled
the nine planets and found

that which unraveled them.
Instead, they passed it down.

*

Can you refuse what is passed down?
You carry it in your gestures, your bones,
the knocking of ghosts, deafening.

They learned the art of destruction
even as they were creating beauty,
admiring texture and color,
entering brilliant vistas.
Wounding and wounded,
they tried. They could not fathom
themselves. All was mystery.

But they loved me in their woundedness,
a cord they could not break.
They tended me. From a great distance,
they cried, *amma, amma*
even if no trunk call had been placed
to alert them I was on death's brink.

They say you cannot do anything
about karma. You simply accept it
and do your best. But I wish
my sons will search and name it.

*

The epics are about searching and naming karma:
Amba fights rejection, turns herself into a man
to kill her rival, Bheeshma.

When a sage's curse hounds Pandu
you will die if you have sex,
his wives bear sons from gods in lieu

of the husband. The queen warns, "Stop!"
when Krishna reaches for a third helping of Sudama's gift
saving his kingdom and his friendship.

Gods seduce mortal wives by trickery,
pose as their husbands, until gods and women
are courted by an angry patriarchy.

✳

I witness an angry patriarchy —
women shake their heads,
Durvasar kopum,

Simile reaching back into the past,
of myth and lore, not merely
the generations I know.

Some say you can change your husband.
I can't say I have tried and failed.
He expected women to bend.

✳

You might ask how he made us bend
to his will. If you had been in a blast
would you avoid it, whether foe or friend?

His furrowed brow, the expostulations
from his lips, the dreaded silence
were the map of his actions

that made me understand the shape of anger
its name, its weight, its wants,
its corrosive edges, its insatiable hunger.

And I decided it is better to feed its open mouth
so I could delve into the shadows by grove
and river to dream than be witness to its filth.

*

Witness anger's filth generation after generation,
imagine the waste, the exhaustion.
As if each male had drunk a potion.

*

I was convinced men had drunk a potion.
It did not come with mother's milk
but was delivered to them by an alien.
I asked a wise foremother the cause
of male anger, its source, the urge
they feel to drink this rasa.

Her eyes like glass, she reflected
a truth already dawning in me.
"Because it hides a weakness."

"Then why do mothers favor males,
  help their anger become a banyan?"
"A mother knows her son's weakness."

  Pushed by instinct, I've watered this tree!
  Its spread, its shade, color, light
  I look at suspiciously.

  ∗

"Your suspicion is good," she reasons.
"Can this be reversed? Can I cut it down?"
I beg her. "You know the answers,"

  she replies, her eyes now closed.
  In her silence, I resolve to you
  in the mother's line, blessed

  with song and invention,
  wake the dormant, cut what you must,
  poison contains its own antidote.

  ∗

  Prarabda karma is poison and antidote,
  I think, when I hear myself and others
  utter this phrase, helpless or fraught

  with danger. Karma is a hungry dog, fierce,
  ready to shred anything, fate that we
  must bear and wait for it to pass,

hollowing us out. Within the cave
of our bodies we know the light
despite the jet grip of its finality.

*

This is my final letter,
dear daughters and daughters-in-law.
When you read this, I will be far.

You know how and where and why,
so instructions I have none.
Look questions in the eye.

See the road I have journeyed
and remember only songs I have sung.
Learn them, keep them, the rest is dust.

DELIRIUM

Relatives wander in and out of my room
I see the phases of the moon from my bed
how much longer I want to ask

but my tongue is stone
tumult of melody   clashing notes
find no outlet

My grandsons sail on the floor singing
Rowrowrowyourboat

This is an open-and-shut case
the doctor straightens up

The men whisper   shadows of women
on the wall   an insistent crying of crows
has someone died

which neighbor can it be
the Gujarati man next door or one of the
Malayalee nurses opposite   the Jewish
woman down the street

Hannah
her friend called out from the boat
to the woman waiting with her grandkids
on the jetty

Midday   the kids are in school
shades are drawn to dim the sun
I want to see the skies redden over the harbor

What was the name of the British company
Husband worked for   my mind's going
it started with an M   Mut mul muk mun
my cheek still stings

                              my breasts hang
on either side of my ribs   my body
a dark tunnel between mouth and cunt

     Oh to feel the colored *kol* in my hand my feet
whipping up dust   my body a feather in the air
Daughter-in-law coaxes a spoon of soup
into my mouth
                              Not yet, not yet
I don't feel the liquid just as I could not taste
Husband's cock that he kept stuffing in my mouth
I should've bitten it off   *You are vile* he said

     I can't move my tongue to make song
my mind is dripping dripping
                              dripping evil
Daughter-in-law scolds *cover yourself properly*
what will people say   as if I am some whore

        Here   look at my big hollow   eleven
kids came out of this

Awaiting Dawn

all is foreign   this street
winding down by the tall compound walls
and opening out to the shore

houses of the spirit by the jetty
phantoms next door   all white
white   white
their singing   lonely

like their tortured god on the cross
boats rocking against a creaking dock
all is foreign   as I sit in my prison

elephants striding up the temple path
mynahs sinking and rising in monsoon wind
rain spilling   scents of youth

fish and gutter reek   I am dry
in a warm bed with no desire to look
at a gray sky meeting a grayer water

all is foreign   even the rats
and my joke that I am a female Gandhi

voices and smells recede
death anchors   walks up to me
you are not foreign

NOTES

[13] "The Long Shadow of Evil" *sita kalyanam vaibogame*
. . . a chant typically sung to bless newlyweds in a Hindu
ceremony.

[31] "Ambi Practices Tamil Vowels on His Slate" This
acrostic poem begins with each of the Tamil vowels, the
pronunciation of which is captured in the words that begin
each line.

[49] "Obliteration" Pregnant women believed in the
superstition that exposure to the solar eclipse would harm
the fetus. So, they confined themselves to a darkened room
until they were past the danger.

[60] "Letter to Sarojini" Sarojini Naidu, the first Indian
poet to publish a volume of poems in English, was called the
Nightingale of India.

[70] "Boat Song" *tha thi thi thai* . . . is a typical percussive
beat in the genre of boat race songs in Kerala.

[73] "Paean to Saraswati" *Aadu paambe* . . . is a popular
folk melody, "Dance, snake; play, snake."

[79] "Onam" Onam is a festival celebrated in Kerala.
Kali, with its short vowel sound has two meanings: a type of
dessert and a game. *Kali*, with the long vowel sound, is the
dark goddess.

[89] "A Meditation on Rain In Ragam Mohanam" notation
as it appears in Carnatic music. In this poem, the notes (Sa
Ri Ga Pa Da) represent the pentatonic scale, its western
classical equivalent being Do Re Me So La.

[90] "After the Funeral" *Oppari* is a mourning song sung by hired mourners.

[104] "Delirium" *Kol* is a colored rod used in group dances in South India.

About the Author

PRAMILA VENKATESWARAN, poet laureate of Suffolk County, Long Island (2013-15), is the author of *Thirtha* (Yuganta Press, 2002), *Behind Dark Waters* (Plain View Press, 2008), *Draw Me Inmost* (Stockport Flats, 2009), *Trace* (Finishing Line Press, 2011), *Thirteen Days to Let Go* (Aldrich Press, 2015), and *Slow Ripening* (Local Gems, 2016). An award-winning poet, she teaches English and Women's Studies at Nassau Community College, New York. Author of numerous essays on poetics as well as creative non-fiction, she is also the 2011 Walt Whitman Birthplace Association Long Island Poet of the Year. She has performed her poems internationally in festivals, such as the Geraldine R. Dodge Poetry Festival and Festival Internacional de Poesia de Granada, and is the co-director of Matwaala: South Asian Diaspora Poetry Festival.

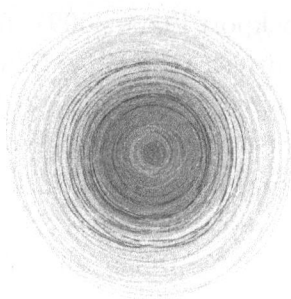

SHANTI ARTS

NATURE ▪ ART ▪ SPIRIT

Please visit us on online
to browse our entire book catalog,
including additional poetry collections and fiction,
books on travel, nature, healing, art,
photography, and more.

www.shantiarts.com

www.ingramcontent.com/pod-product-compliance
Lightning Source LLC
Chambersburg PA
CBHW072357090426
42741CB00012B/3057